BAR GAMES

BAR GAMES

A Guide To Playing
NTN and MEGATOUCH
at Your Favorite Bar or Restaurant

Lauren Shilling

New Chapter Press

Cover and interior design: Emily Brackett, Visible Logic, Chicago, IL
Cover photo: BananaStock

Published by New Chapter Press
ISBN 0-94225-737-5
Printed in the United States of America

Table of Contents

Introduction

A very familiar sight in bars across America is a television screen displaying the NTN® logo. A NTN trivia game is in progress, testing the skills of many of the bar's patrons. They seem to be having a lot of fun, trying to achieve a high score in the game that links thousands of establishments together via satellite TV signal.

At the end of the bar, there is a MEGATOUCH®. It looks like a computer monitor with a small keyboard. Likely that the game is being played by a couple, testing each others skills in one of the many games offered on this machine.

These games have changed the landscape of many bars across America. The ambience is enhanced by an additional level of conviviality.

This book, BAR GAMES, describes techniques to improve your ability to achieve a high score in these games. Playing techniques are described. A large section of trivia is included, covering subjects used in the NTN game and in the trivia related MEGATOUCH games.

NTN® is a trademark of NTN Communications, Carlsbad, CA.
MEGATOUCH® is a trademark of Merit Industries, Reading, PA.

NTN Trivia Game

NTN Trivia Game

Almost the national sport, NTN is played by young and old in over 10,000 restaurants, bars and cocktail lounges in the US and Canada. These places are linked together via satellite to the NTN central computer in California.

The familiar NTN logo, appearing on a one or more TV sets, signifies the present of the game in that establishment and the presence of intelligent, competitive players there.

Ask the hostess or bartender for a game playing board, sign on, and compete with the 40,000 people who are usually playing at cocktail time. The game playing board is a small keyboard where answers are entered. It is wireless and battery powered. Enter your nickname and enter the nationwide competition.

Best to register so you can accumulate points that some places use to give discounts on food. Pick out a nickname and you are on-line via the magic of a satellite which transmits questions to each location and receives and retransmits answers to the central NTN computer.

Game Description
The normal game consists of a question followed by the display of five possible answers. An immediate answer will give you a score of 1000. The score value decreases

Q: Who was the only bachelor President?

down to zero in about 60 seconds. Two clues are displayed indicating which answers are not correct followed by the clue usually indicating the correct answer.

Playing Methodology and Strategy

If you know the answer, enter it, hope you are correct, and wait to be awarded 1000 points. If you do not know the answer, guess at one of the answers, hit that button on the game board, and watch the clues. If the first clue indicates that your answer is wrong, take another guess. If the second clue indicates that that answer is wrong too, guess again.

Guessing is the correct strategy as you have a 20% chance of being correct on the first guess and getting 1000 points.

The second guess after an incorrect first guess still offers a 25% chance of being correct with a good score of about 600 points.

Watch out for a negative clues which are frequently given as the last clue to fool the player.

For example, a question might be as follows:

WHO APPEARED IN THE FIRST 'TALKING' MOTION PICTURE?

Possible Answers:

1. AL JOLSON
2. FATTY ARBUCKLE
3. THE THREE STOOGES
4. GRETA GARBO
5. THE MARX BROTHERS

Clues:

1. NOT GRETA
2. NOT FATTY

Usually the third clue would be:

IT's AL

But a negative clue would be:

NOT THE THREE

Some players automatically enter the name on the last clue, Three Stooges. Wrong. The Answer is Al Jolson and the movie was "The Jazz Age". Do not take the clue if there is a 'NOT' in front of the last clue.

The NTN company is based in California so many questions are movie or TV program related. The games vary by time and day of the week. Certain time slots have history related questions, geography, artists, authors, etc. There is a game for everyone, but all games are fun to play as long as you do not mind getting a low score for a game in a category which is not your specialty. About fifteen 30 minute games are played each night.

Q: Name the Capital of North Dakota.

These are some of the games that are featured on NTN:

Sports IQ
Sports related questions. A real challenge for serious sports fans.

Passport
Questions on far away places, sites to see there, travel, etc.

The Sci-files
Trivia questions on science fiction TV programs and books.

Brain Buster
Very difficult questions of an intellectual nature. Difficult clues as well.

Sports Trivia Challenge
Questions about sports figures, including coaches, players, owners. Note that there are frequently questions on Canadian sports because of the large number of NTN players in Canada.

Triviaoke®
Questions in this game involve song lyrics and the completion of familiar Quotations. Triviaoke is a play on words (Karaoke and Trivia)

Triviaoke® is a trademark of NTN Communications, Carlsbad, CA.

Topix
Several categories of questions in this game, one of which is about cast members in motion pictures from The 1970's and 1980's.

Abused News
Humorous questions on current news events. A favorite of many players.

Retroactive
Questions involving TV shows from the 1960's and 1970's.

Pick Six
Six names are listed on the left of the screen. Six categories are listed on the right. The names on the left are to be matched with categories on the right. Usually, a player knows 4 of the 6 names, the other two are unknown. Best to identify the two you do not know the answer to. When the name on the left is highlighted, the player then selects a number identifying the answer on the right. Very important to guess on the one you do not know. Be sure to use each answer only once. Do not guess the same answer twice.

Many other games are offered. The web site, www.ntn.com, displays a schedule of the times that these games are offered in the four North American time zones.

Q: Charlemagne began his reign in what year?

Trivia — Introduction

Trivia, according the Webster's Unabridged, are "matters or things that are very important, inconsequential, or nonessential". The word is always plural, like a potato chip. You can't have just one.

The Latin root of our favorite pastime turns out to be "trivium" (yes, the word for one trivia) and that breaks down into 'three' as in triplex, and vium, meaning way.

Trivia, in the days when Nero was still fiddling, meant "the place where three roads meet".

And how does that relate to "matters... that are very unimportant"? Because crossroads to Romans were where guys hung out and talked about, well, trivia.

But wait! It gets even better. In a definition of trivia found online at www.Hyperdictionary.com, a synonym is "small beer". (Synonym means the same as in case you slept through seventh grade English).

Street corners! Small beer! Wasting time! Home at last!

So here it is on the following pages: Presidents And Their Veeps, Mushrooms, Wine, Oscar Wilde, Lakes , Rivers, Seinfeld's Address, Authors, History, Artists, Roman Numerals, Henry VIII, and Jack The Ripper.

Enjoy!

Q: What is the Roman numeral for 500?

Time Lines – What Happened When!

I was a 'C' student in history and always seek help on NTN
history questions. In compiling this section on history, I
sought the help of the local history expert at Fast Eddie's
on K Street in Washington, Justin. He plays NTN trivia
under the name "TURBO", works on Capitol Hill for one
of the congressional committees and enjoys the history
questions on NTN.

Turbo spent a few nights making up the following time line
list of dates which is very helpful to NTN players.

Turbo is a regular for the history related games, sitting
at the bar, with his NTN board, a MillerLite® and a small
pizza. On these games, Turbo is frequently listed with the
national leaders posted after the game by NTN.

MillerLite® is a trademark of the Miller Brewing Company, Milwaukee, WI.

BC

NOTE: BC meaning "Before Christ" was the common description of these dates until recently when BCE meaning "Before Common Era" replaced it.

1,000,000	**2690-2180**	**1550-1070**	**Uncertain**	**480-430**
Dinosaur era ends	Eqyptian Old Kingdom (pyramids at Giza built)	Eqyptian New Kingdom (King Tut reigns 1342-1323)	Trojan War: Greek City State, Athens vs. Troy (in Turkey) Myth mixed with reality	Golden Age of Pericles in Greece
	2000-1700 Eqyptian Middle Kingdom			

Q: Who wrote "Gone With The Wind"?

323
Alexander The Great dies at age 33 after conquering most of the civilized world

approximately 300
Second Jewish Temple started in Jerusalem

260
First Punic War (Rome vs. Carthage)

218
Second Punic War (Hannibal crossed Alps with Elephants to attack Rome)

216
Battle of Cannae Roman troops enveloped by Carthaginians

149-146
Third Punic War (Carthage destroyed)

49
Julius Caesar crossed Rubicon causing Roman Civil War

44
Julius Caesar assassinated by Brutus and others on the Ides of March (March 15)

0
Jesus of Nazareth born in Bethlehem

Major Events Starting With The
Birth Of Jesus

NOTE: AD means anno Domini or "year of our Lord" in Latin. With the emergence of BCE, the corresponding term is CE.

00
Birth of Jesus of Nazareth

27
Jesus Crucified

70
Second Jewish Temple destroyed by Rome

100
Roman Emperor Hadrian builds wall between Scotland and England

300
Constantine adapts Christianity as Roman Religion

407
Alaric The Visigoth sacks Rome

732
Charles Martell defeats Muslim invaders at Tours, France

800
Charlemagne begins 14 year reign as Holy Roman Emperor

1066
Norman Invasion, Battle of Hastings, and conquest of Saxons in Great Britain

1085
Doomsday Book written in England for William the Conqueror (Great Britain census)

Q: When was Louis XVI guillotined?

1095
First Crusade
initiated by
Pope Urban II

1154
First and only
English Pope,
Adrian IV,
elected

1181
Saint Francis,
founder of
Franciscan
Order, born in
Assissi

1203
4th Crusade -
Constantinople
Sacked by
Christian
Crusaders

1271
Marco Polo,
aged 17,
begins travels
to China with
family

1297
Magna Carta
signed by
Edward I –
rights
guaranteed to
the populace

1337
One Hundred
Years War
begins
(England vs
France)

1347
Bubonic
plague begins
in Europe
(kills 1/3
of population

1386
Donatello born
in Florence
(foremost
Sculptor
of Era)

1455-85
War of The
Roses (House
of Lancaster
vs House of
York—both
had roses in
their crest)

1483
Raphael
(Raffaello
Sanzio), artist
of renown,
born in Urbino

1492
Columbus
Discovers
America

1498
Savonarola,
religious
reformer,
burned at
stake in
Florence

1503
Leonardo,
born 1452,
paints Mona
Lisa, now in
The Louvre

1511
Michelangelo,
born 1475,
finishes
painting Sistine
Chapel

1607
Jamestown
Virginia Colony
founded

1620
Pilgrims Land
at Plymouth
Rock

1692
First Salem
witch, Sarah
Prince
Osborne,
convicted and
dies in Boston
Prison

Q: Who painted The Last Supper?

1702-13
Queen Anne's War (English vs French/ Spanish known in Europe as The War of The Spanish Succession)

1726
Scotch-Irish Immigration to America underway (John Walker lands in Maryland)

1756
French & Indian War (colonies versus French & Indians)

1769
James Watt invents the Steam Engine in Scotland

1781
American Revolution, started in 1776, ends by defeat of Cornwallis at Yorktown, VA

1789
French Revolution starts

1793
Louis XVI guillotined

1805
Napoleon defeated in Russia

1807
Robert Fulton sails steamboat from NY to Albany

1812
War of 1812

1814	**1825**	**1846**	**1865**	**1898**
Napoleon exiled to Elba	Erie Canal completed– NY City booms on trade for midwest	Mexican War starts	American Civil War, begun in 1861, at Ft. Sumter, ends	Spanish American War
1815		**1848**		**1914**
Napoleon defeated at Waterloo by Wellington and Bruche and exiled to St. Helena		Potato Famine in Ireland Vast Irish immigration to USA	**1870** Franco- Prussian War (Bismarck unites German States)	World War I starts after assassination of Austrian heir, Franz Ferdinand and his wife, Sofia, In Sarajevo
	1837 Great Depression of 1837			

Q: In what year did Apollo land on the moon?

1918
Russian Tsar
Nicholas II
and family
assassinated

1918
World War
I ends with
Armistice on
November 11

1929
Stock Market
Crash in New
York Great
Depression
begins

1936
Spanish Civil
War starts.
Generalissimo
Franco vs.
Loyalists
(Reds)

1939
Germany
attacks Poland,
starting World
War II

1941
Japanese
attack Pearl
Harbor
December 7

August 1945
Atomic bombs
dropped on
Hiroshima
and Nagasaki,
ending WW
II. Cold War
begins

1948
Israel created,
Arab-Jewish
war begins.

1950
Korean War
begins

1953
French
defeated in
Indo-China

1963
Martin Luther
King 'I have a
dream speech'
Washington
DC

1963
JFK
assassinated
by Lee Harvey
Oswald

1964
Vietnam War
starts

1968
Robert
Kennedy
assassinated
by Sirhan
Basrah Sirhan

1968
Martin
Luther King
assassinated
by James Earl
Ray

1974
Nixon resigns

1982
British-
Argentina
War over the
Maldives
(Falklands)

1990
Gulf War

1993
World Trade
Center
Explosion

**September 11,
2001**
World Trade
Center
destroyed by
hijacked plane

March 2003
Iraq invaded
by US led
Coalition

Q: How did Anne Boleyn, Henry VIII's wife, die?

Presidents
of the United States

Name	Birthplace	Residence	
1. Washington, George	Colony of VA	VA	
2. Adams, John	Colony of MA	MA	
3. Jefferson, Thomas	Colony of VA	VA	
4. Madison, James	Colony of MA	VA	
5. Monroe, James	Colony of VA	VA	VA Senator
6. Adams, John Quincy	Colony of MA	MA	Monroe's Secy of State
7. Jackson, Andrew	Colony of NC	TN	War of 1812 General
8. Van Buren, Martin	NY	NY	In Jackson's cabinet

Van Buren was the first President actually born in the United States! Prior Presidents were born when the USA was a British Colony.

9. Harrison, William Henry	VA	IN	Governor of IN
10. Tyler, John	VA	VA	First VP to be president
11. Polk, James K.	NC	TN	Congressman from TN
12. Taylor, Zachary	VA	MS	Mexican War General
13. Fillmore, Millard	NY	NY	Succeeded from Vice President upon death of Taylor
14. Pierce, Franklin	NH	NH	NH Senator
15. Buchanan, James	PA	PA	PA Senator and Polk's Secretary of State Only bachelor President.

Name	Birthplace	Residence	
16. Lincoln, Abraham	KY	IL	Served one term as Congressman
17. Johnson, Andrew	NC	TN	TN Senator
18. Grant, Ulysses S.	OH	OH	Civil War Union General
19 Hayes, Rutherford B.	OH	OH	He did not get majority of vote
20. Garfield, James A.	OH	OH	Ohio Senator
21. Arthur, Chester A.	VT	NY	VP – became President when Garfield assassinated
22. Cleveland, Grover	NJ	NY	NY Governor
23. Harrison, Benjamin	OH	IN	Senator from Indiana
24. Cleveland, Grover	NJ	NY	Married in White House
25. McKinley, William	OH	OH	Congressman, OH Governor
26. Roosevelt, Theodore	NY	NY	NY Governor - McKinley's VP – succeeded when McKinley was assassinated)
27. Taft, William Howard	OH	OH	Roosevelt's Secretary of War
28. Wilson, Woodrow	VA	NJ	NJ Governor
29. Harding, Warren	OH	OH	Governor of Ohio
30. Coolidge, Calvin	VT	MA	MA Governor
31. Hoover, Herbert	IA		Coolidge's Secretary of Commerce
32. Roosevelt, Franklin D.	NY	NY	Governor of NY
33. Truman, Harry S.	MO	MO	Senator from MO
34. Eisenhower, Dwight D	TX	NY	President of Columbia U.
35. Kennedy, John F	MA	MA	MA Senator
36. Johnson, Lyndon B.	TX	TX	TX Senator
37. Nixon, Richard M.	CA	CA	CA Senator
38. Ford, Gerry	MI	MI	MI Congressman

Q: When was Napoleon defeated at Waterloo?

Name	Birthplace	Residence	
39. Carter, James	GA	GA	GA Governor
40. Reagan, Ronald	IL	CA	First divorced President
41. Bush, George	CT	TX	TX Congressman
42. Clinton, William	AR	AR	AR Governor
43. Bush, George	TX	TX	TX Governor

Addenda

James K. Polk's wife, Sarah, banned 'hard liquor' from the White House. She did serve fine wine and ' home brew'. Rumor has it that Sarah was heard saying, "MillerLite®, where are you now that I need you".

William Henry Harrison was the first President to die in office, of pneumonia, one month after being inaugurated.

College Presidents

Eisenhower	Columbia U. (NY City)
Wilson	Princeton U. (NJ)
Garfield	Hiram College (OH)

Vice Presidents
Of The United States Of America

President	Vice President
Washington	John Adams
Adams	Thomas Jefferson
Jefferson	Aaron Burr
Jefferson	George Clinton
Madison	George Clinton
Monroe	Daniel Tompkins
Adams	John Calhoun
Jackson	John Calhoun
Jackson	Martin Van Buren
Van Buren	Richard Johnson
Harrison	John Tyler
Polk	George Dallas
Taylor	Millard Fillmore
Pierce	William King
Buchanan	John Breckinridge (Youngest at age 36)
Lincoln	Hannibal Hamlin
Lincoln	Andrew Johnson
Johnson	-
Grant	Schuyler Colfax
Grant	Henry Wilson
Hayes	William Wheeler
Garfield	Chester Arthur
Cleveland	Adlai Stevenson
McKinley	Garrett Hobart

Q: Which planet is farthest from the Sun?

President	Vice President
McKinley	Theodore Roosevelt
Roosevelt	Charles Fairbanks
Taft	James Sherman
Wilson	Thomas Marshall
Harding	Calvin Coolidge
Coolidge	Charles Gates Dawes
Hoover	Charles Curtis
Roosevelt	Janes Nance Garner
Roosevelt	Henry Wallace
Roosevelt	Harry Truman
Truman	Alben Barkley
Eisenhower	Richard Nixon
Kennedy	Lyndon Johnson
Johnson	Hubert Humphrey
Nixon	Spiro Agnew
Nixon	Gerald Ford
Ford	Nelson Rockefeller
Carter	Walter Mondale
Reagan	George Bush
Bush	J. Danforth Quayle
Clinton	Albert Gore
Bush	Richard Cheney

Those Who Died In Office

George Clinton	(Jefferson)
Henry Wilson	(Grant)
Thomas Hendricks	(Cleveland)
Garret Hobart	(McKinley)
James Sherman	(Taft)

Those Who Later Became President

John Adams	(Washington)	elected
Martin Van Buren	(Jackson)	elected
Millard Fillmore	(Taylor)	death of Taylor
Andrew Johnson	(Lincoln)	death of Lincoln
Chester Arthur	(Garfield)	death of Garfield
Theodore Roosevelt	(McKinley)	death of McKinley
Calvin Coolidge	(Harding)	death of Harding
Harry Truman	(Roosevelt)	death of Roosevelt
Lyndon Johnson	(Kennedy)	death of Kennedy
Gerald Ford	(Nixon)	resignation of Nixon
George H. W. Bush	(Reagan)	elected

Those Who Became Senators After Vice Presidential Term

John Calhoun
John Breckinridge
Hannibal Hamlin
Andrew Johnson
Alben Barkley
Hubert Humphrey

Q: What river is the longest?

Those Who Resigned

Spiro Agnew resigned when it was discovered he was dishonest.

John C. Calhoun resigned on the insistence of his wife, Floride, who objected to being in the company of Peggy Eaton, the wife of a cabinet member, John Eaton. Peggy Eaton was thought to be a women of loose virtue.

Floride, a hard women, worthy of her name!

The **United Kingdom**
of Great Britain

Monarchs

Elizabeth II	1952-present	
George VI	1936-1952	Edward VIII's younger brother
Edward VIII	1936	He abdicated to marry a twice divorced American, Wallis Warfield Simpson.
George V	1910-1936	He changed the family name in 1917 to Windsor from Saxe-Coburg-Gotha due to anti-German feeling in England
Edward VII	1901-1910	Edward VII's girl friend was Alice Keppel. Alice's great granddaughter, Camilla Parker Bowes, is the girl friend of Prince Charles. (The family has the girl friend gene!)
Victoria	1837-1901	Husband was Prince Albert, a German
William IV	1830-1837	
George IV	1820-1830	
George III	1760-1820	Made famous by the American Revolution. He suffered from Porphyria (neurological disorder) and was insane most of his life.
George II	1727-1760	

Q: Who was assassinated on the Ides of March?

George I	1714-1727	Born in Hanover, Germany, in 1660. He spent most of his time there and never learned to speak English!
Anne	1702-1714	Queen Anne's War prevented alliance between France and Spain
William III & Mary II	1689-1702	William, from Holland, married his first cousin Mary, for political reasons – William & Mary College is named for them.
James II	1685-1688	
Charles II	1680-1685	
Richard Cromwell	1658-1659	
Oliver Cromwell	1649-1658	He led parliamentary army against an unruly King Charles, overthrowing him
Charles I	1625-1649	(Oliver deposed him!)
James I	1603-1625	Sponsored scholars in creation of the King James version of the Bible
Elizabeth I	1558-1603	
Mary I	1553-1558	
Lady Jane Grey	1553	reigned for nine days until the legitimacy of Mary was determined
Edward VI	1547-1553	
Henry VIII	1509-1547	See Chapter on him, page 49.
Henry VII	1485-1509	
Richard III	1483-1485	The murderer of Edward V Shakespeare's play, "Richard III", Is about this episode
Edward V	1483	Reigned for two months before being deposed and murdered, along with his brother, in the Tower of London.

Edward IV	1461-1483	
Henry VI	1422-1461	
Henry V	1413-1422	
Henry IV	1399-1413	
Richard II	1377-1399	
Edward III	1327-1377	
Edward II	1307-1327	His wife, plotting against him, arranged for his execution.
Edward I	1272-1307	
Henry III	1216-1272	
John	1199-1216	
Richard (The Lionhearted)	1189-1199	Led the Third Crusade. Little time spent in England (lucky citizens).
Henry II	1154-1189	
Matilda	1141	Seized the throne for one year. Never crowned
Stephen	1135-1154	
Henry I	1100-1135	
William II	1087-1100	
William I (The Conqueror)	1066-1087	A Frenchman from Normandy invaded and conquered Britain. The Pope gave him permission to do so as he was related to previous monarchs.

Q: Name the grape used to make Champagne.

Henry VIII — English King

Good ole Henry, frequently the subject of trivia questions appearing in the NTN game. Born in 1491, He had six wives. It is likely he occasionally forgot their names and what happened to them!

So we have a little poem to help us to remember.

> Divorced, Beheaded, Died;
> Divorced, Beheaded, Survived

Their names:

Catherine of Aragon	Divorced *(lucky her)*
Anne Boleyn	Beheaded *(not so lucky)*
Jane Seymour	Died
Anne of Cleves	Divorced
Catherine Howard	Beheaded *(another one)*
Catherine Parr	Survived

Henry's behavior was looked upon by disfavor by The Roman Catholic Church who excommunicated him.

Too bad MillerLite® was not available at that time. Perhaps it would have mellowed him a bit.

MillerLite® is a trademark of the Miller Brewing Company, Milwaukee, WI.

The **States** Of The Union

Questions about States are frequently asked in trivia games. Here is a list of the states with their nickname and capitol.

State	Nickname	Capitol City
Alabama	Yellowhammer State	Montgomery
Alaska	Last Frontier	Juneau
Arizona	Grand Canyon State	Phoenix
Arkansas	Opportunity State	Little Rock
California	Golden State	Sacramento
Colorado	Centennial State	Denver

Q: Who wrote "The Sun Also Rises"?

State	Nickname	Capitol City
Connecticut	Nutmeg State	Hartford
Delaware	Blue Hen State	Dover
Florida	Citrus State	Tallahassee
Georgia	Peach State	Atlanta
Hawaii	Aloha State	Honolulu
Illinois	Prairie State	Springfield
Idaho	Gem State	Boise
Indiana	Hoosier State	Indianapolis
Iowa	Hawkeye State	Des Moines
Kansas	Sunflower State	Topeka
Kentucky	Blue Grass State	Frankfort
Louisiana	none	Baton Rouge
Maine	Pine Tree State	Augusta
Maryland	Old Line State	Annapolis
Massachusetts	Bay State	Boston
Michigan	Wolverine State	Lansing
Minnesota	North Star State	St. Paul
Missouri	Show Me State	Jefferson City
Mississippi	Magnolia State	Jackson
Montana	Treasure State	Helena
Nebraska	Cornhusker State	Lincoln
Nevada	Silver State	Carson City
New Hampshire	Granite State	Concord
New Jersey	Garden State	Trenton
New Mexico	Land of Enchantment	Sante Fe
New York	Empire State	Albany
North Carolina	Tar Heel State	Raleigh
North Dakota	Roughrider State	Bismarck

State	Nickname	Capitol City
Ohio	Buckeye State	Columbus
Oklahoma	Sooner State	Oklahoma City
Oregon	Beaver State	Salem
Pennsylvania	Keystone State	Harrisburg
Rhode Island	Ocean State	Providence
South Carolina	Palmetto State	Columbia
South Dakota	Mt. Rushmore State	Pierre
Tennessee	Volunteer State	Nashville
Texas	Lone Star State	Austin
Utah	Beehive State	Salt Lake City
Vermont	Green Mountain State	Montpelier
Virginia	Old Dominion State	Richmond
Washington	Evergreen State	Olympia
West Virginia	Mountain State	Charleston
Wisconsin	Badger State	Madison
Wyoming	Equality State	Cheyenne

Q: Name the world's largest lake. (Called a sea)

More Facts

Montana has the lowest population density, less than one person per square mile.

Wyoming was the first state to let women vote.

Rhode Island was the last state to ratify the constitution.

The **original 13** states were:

Delaware
Georgia
Maine
Massachusetts
New Hampshire
New Jersey
New York
North Carolina
Maryland
Pennsylvania
Rhode Island
South Carolina
Virginia

The Twenty **Largest Natural Lakes** On Earth

Listed By Surface Area

Lake	Surface Area (In Square Miles)
1. Caspian Sea	143,244
2. Lake Superior	31,700
3. Lake Victoria	28,828
4. Lake Huron	23,000
5. Lake Michigan	22,300
6. Aral Sea	13,000
7. Lake Tanganyika	12,700
8. Lake Baykal	12,162
9. Great Bear Lake	12,096
10. Nyasa Lake	11,150
11. Great Slave Lake	11,031
12. Lake Erie	9,910
13. Winnipeg	9,417
14. Lake Ontario	7,340
15. Lake Balkhash	7,115
16. Lake Ladoga	6,835
17. Lake Maracaibo	5,217
18. Lake Onega	3,710
19. Lake Eyre	3,600
20. Lake Titicaca	3,200

Lake Superior #2
Lake Huron #4
Lake Ontario #14
Lake Michigan #5
Lake Erie #12

Great Lakes Of The United States (Also Listed Above)

Lake Superior	31,700
Lake Huron	23,000
Lake Michigan	22,300
Lake Erie	9,910
Lake Ontario	7,340

Q: Who was the first Vice President?

Rivers Of The World

Listed According to length

Name	Length (Miles)	Destination
Nile	4150	Mediterranean Sea
Amazon	4000	Atlantic Ocean
Yangtze (Chang)	3964	East China Sea
Mississippi/Missouri	3710	Gulf of Mexico
Yellow (Huang)	3395	Yellow Sea
Ob-Intysh	3362	Gulf of Ob (Arctic Ocean)
Congo	2900	Atlantic Ocean
Volga	2790	Caspian Sea
Lena	2734	Laptov Sea (Arctic Ocean)
Mekong	2700	South China Sea
Niger	2590	Gulf of Guinea
Parana	2485	Rio de la Plata (Atlantic Ocean)

Rivers Of North America

Name	Length (Miles)	Destination
Mississippi/Missouri	3710	Gulf of Mexico
Columbia/Snake	2000	Pacific Ocean
Yukon	1979	Bering Sea
Rio Grande	1800	Gulf of Mexico
Colorado	1450	Gulf of California
Ohio/Allegheny	1300	Mississippi River
Mackenzie River	1060	Arctic Ocean
Churchill River	900	Hudson Bay (renamed 1965 formerly Hamilton river)

The **Twenty Largest Cities**
in the World, Listed By Population

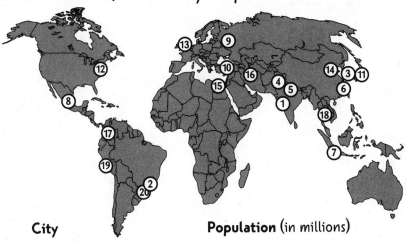

	City	Population (in millions)
1.	Bombay, India	11.9
2.	Sao Paulo, Brazil	10.4
3.	Seoul, South Korea	9.9
4.	Karachi, Pakistan	9.8
5.	Delhi, India	9.8
6.	Shanghai, China	9.2
7.	Jakarta, Indonesia	9.1
8.	Mexico City, Mexico	8.5
9.	Moscow, Russia	8.4
10.	Istanbul, Turkey	8.1
11.	Tokyo, Japan	8.1
12.	New York City, USA	8.0
13.	London, United Kingdom	7.2
14.	Beijing, China	6.9
15.	Cairo, Egypt	6.9
16.	Teheran, Iran	6.7
17.	Bogota, Columbia	6.7
18.	Bangkok, Thailand	6.3
19.	Lima, Peru	6.2
20.	Rio de Janeiro, Brazil	5.8

Q: Who sacked Rome in 407 AD?

World Cities Listed by
Latitude

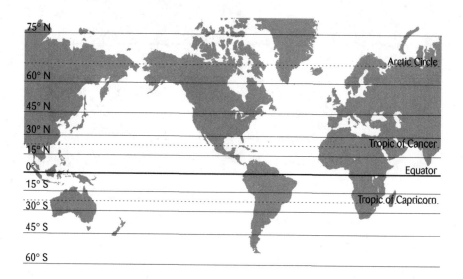

Northern Hemisphere – Northern most first.

Name	Latitude	
Reykjavik	64:04	
Anchorage	61:00	
Helsinki	60:10	
Oslo	59:57	
Stockholm	59:17	
Edinburgh	55:55	(Edinburgh warmer than Moscow; warmed by Gulf stream Current of the Atlantic Ocean)
Moscow	55:45	
Berlin	52:30	

London	51:32
Prague	50:05
Paris	48:48
Vienna	48:14
Seattle	47:00
Montreal	45:30
Minneapolis	44:00
Toronto	43:40
Boston	42:00
Detroit	42:00
Rome	41:54
Chicago	41:00
New York	40:00
Philadelphia	39:00
Washington DC	39:00
St. Louis	38:00
Athens	37:58
Los Angeles	33:00
Phoenix	33:00
Cairo	30:02
Miami	25:00
Honolulu	21:18
Singapore	1:14

Southern Hemisphere — Southern most first.

Name	Latitude
Melbourne	37:47
Sydney	34:00
Capetown	33:55
Perth	31:57
Johannesburg	26:12
Rio de Janeiro	22:57
Mexico City	19:26
Lima	12:00
Jakarta	6:16
Bogata	4:32
Nairobi	1:25

Q: Who was the first Salem witch?

NASA History

There are many questions regarding the NASA space program on NTN. Best to remember some of this.

NASA, The National Aeronautics and Space Administration, was founded in 1958 to initiate the USA's space exploration program. Starting with the Mercury program, which was a small, unmanned satellite, NASA has progressed thru sub-orbital manned missions, such as the Mercury mission of Allan Shepard, to the moon exploration with Apollo.

Rockets of increasing size and complexity have been developed over the years to place these satellites in orbit and beyond. The first rocket used was the Redstone, followed by the Atlas, Titan, and Saturn.

Time Line

1961, May	Mercury suborbital flight – Alan Shepard
1965, June	Gemini – First Space Walk – Edward White
1968, Oct.	Apollo 7 orbits moon
1969, July	Apollo 11 lands on the moon Crew: Neil Armstrong, Edwin Aldrin, Michael Collins
1972-73	Pioneer 10 and 11, unmanned spacecraft, travel to Jupiter to collect scientific data
1973	Apollo programs ends after 6 Lunar landings
1975	Apollo-Sayuz USA-Soviet Russia joint mission
1977	Voyager 1 and 2 tour the Solar System
1981	First Shuttle vehicle launched
1986, Jan.	Challenger spacecraft crashes on lift off Crew: Sharon McAuliffe, Judith Resnick, Gregory Jarvis, Ellison Onizuka, Ronald McNair, Francis Scobee, Michael Smith
1992, May	Space Shuttle Endeavor makes first flight
1998	MIR space station launched—Astronauts live there for an extended period
1990	Hubble Space Telescope launched—does not function
1997, June	Pathfinder Robot lands on Mars
2000, Feb.	NEAR spacecraft begins examination of asteroid, Eros, with a close orbit. (NASA Discovery Program)
2002	Hubble Advanced Telescope relays pictures to Earth of distant galaxies.
2003	Columbia Space Shuttle explodes on re-entry to Earth's atmosphere

Q: Which of the USA's Great Lakes is the largest?

Planets

Ordered from the closest to the sun to the farthest away.
Diameter is in miles.

Name	Diameter	Satellites
Mercury	3,030	none
Venus	7,515	none
Earth	7,921	Moon
Mars	4,219	2, Phobos and Demos
Jupiter	88,793	40, Sinope is largest
Saturn	74,732	30, Phoebe is largest
Uranus	31,693	20, Setebos is largest
Neptune	30,759	1, Nereid is largest
Pluto	1,412	1, Charon

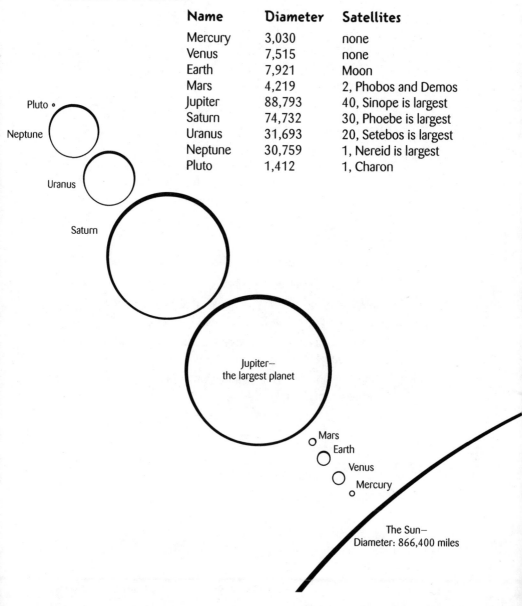

Pluto

Neptune

Uranus

Saturn

Jupiter—
the largest planet

Mars

Earth

Venus

Mercury

The Sun—
Diameter: 866,400 miles

Colors Of The Rainbow

Remembered by a man's name, ROY G. BIV

Red
Orange
Yellow
Green
Blue
Indigo
Violet

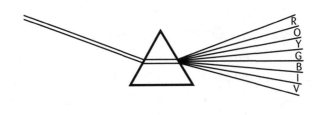

Q: When did World War I end?

Painters

Questions regarding artists and art of frequently included in NTN games. He is some information about this subject.

An Overview Of Classical Art
Schools of Art: In the context of classical art, a 'school' defines a certain style, interest, and/or period of time of the work.

The most well know schools of art are as follows:

Dutch School (Rembrandt)

Realism

Impressionism (Defined by first impressionist painting "Impressionism Sunrise" - Claude Monet 1872)

Post Impressionism

Expressionism

Cubism

Fauvism

New York School (Abstract Impressionism - Jackson Pollock et al)

Artists Grouped By Category

Surrealists

Max Ernst	1891-1976	Germany
Salvador Dali	1904-1989	Spain
Joan Miro	1893-1983	Spain

Cubists

Pablo Picasso	1881-1973	Spain
Paul Cezanne	1839-1906	France
George Braque	1882-1963	France

Abstract Impressionists - New York School

Ad Reinhardt	1913-1967	USA
Jackson Pollock	1912-1956	USA
Mark Rothko	1903-1970	Russia
Robert Motherwell	1915-1991	USA
Larry Poons	1937	

Hudson River School

Frederick Church	1826-1900	USA
Albert Bierstadt	1830-1902	Germany
James A. Suydam	1819-1865	USA
J. F. Cropsey	1823-1900	USA
V. Degrailly	1804-1889	France

Q: Who was the first President born in The United States of America?

Impressionists

Frederic Bazille	1841-1870	France
Mary Cassatt	1844-1926	USA
Jean-Baptiste-Camille Corot	1796-1875	France
Edgar Degas	1834-1917	France
Edouardo Manet	1832-1883	France
Claude Monet	1840-1926	France
Camille Pissaro	1830-1903	West Indies
August Renoir	1841-1919	France
Alfred Sisley	1839-1899	France

Note: Sisley's parents were English.

Mary Cassatt was a rich American ex-patriate. Her father was President of the Pennsylvania Railroad, which was the largest corporation in America at that time. She was invited to show with the Impressionists by her friend, Edgar Degas.

Edgar Degas lived in 1872-1873 in New Orleans. His studio there is now a Bed and Breakfast Guest House.

Post Impressionists

Paul Cezanne	1839-1906	France
Paul Gauguin	1848-1903	France
Vincent Van Gogh	1853-1910	Holland (close friend of Gauguin)
Henri Toulouse-Lautrec	1864-1901	
Edouard Vuillard	1868-1910	France (Also considered a Symbolist)

Realists

George Bellows	1882-1925	USA
Gustave Courbet	1819-1877	France
Winslow Homer	1836-1910	USA
Edouard Manet	1832-1883	France

Expressionists

Amadeo Modigliani	1884-1909	Italy
Paul Klee	1879-1940	Switzerland

Fauvists (An art critic gave them this title, meaning 'From Wild Beasts')

Henri Matisse	1869-1954	France
Maurice de Vlaminck	1876-1958	France

Old Masters - Various Schools

Sandro Botticelli	1445-1510	Born in Florence
Leonardo Da Vinci	1452-1519	Mona Lisa, The Last Supper
Gerard David Bruges	1460-1523	
Hans Holbein The Elder	1465-1524	
Michelangelo	1475-1564	High renaissance painter- Sistine Chapel
Titian	1485-1576	Foremost painter of the Venetian School
Hans Holbein The Younger	1497-1543	A friend of Sir Thomas More and Erasmus)
Jacopo Tintoretto	1518-1594	Venetian School
El Greco	1541-1614	Domenikos Theotocopoulous "The Greek" painted in Spain
Carravaggio	1573-1610	

Q: Which President was the first to die in office?

Sir Anthony Van Dyck	1599-1641	Baroque artist - pupil of Rubens. Spent the last years of his life in England as court artist for Charles I. Knighted by the Crown.
Peter Paul Rubens	1577-1640	Flemish Baroque artist
Diego Velazguez	1599-1660	Spanish Court artist
Rembrandt Van Rijn	1606-1669	Born in Leiden, died in Amsterdam. Dutch School
Thomas Gainsborough	1727-1788	English landscape and portrait artist
Jacques-Louis David	1748-1825	French neoclassicist -left France when Napoleon was exiled
J.M.W. Turner	1775-1851	English landscape and marine artist
Jean-Auguste-Dominique Ingres	1780-1867	pupil of David

Miscellaneous

James Whistler 1834 (USA)-1903

James Whistler was an American ex-patriate. Born in the USA, he lived in St. Petersburg, Russia, as a teenager where his father was employed by the Czar, building the Russian railway system. He attended West Point for two years. Upon dismissal from West Point, he worked for the US Bureau of Engraving. His work was varied. Some etchings, portraits, 'Whistlers Mother', his most famous painting, impressionist works, etc. "The Picture of Dorian Gray", by Oscar Wilde, is loosely modeled on Whistler who was Wilde's friend (and later enemy).

Walter Sickert 1860 (England)-1942
He has been accused by American author, Patricia Cornwell, of being "Jack The Ripper".

John Singer Sargent 1856 (Italy)-1925
A portraitist, he also was a noted Impressionist. Born in Florence, Italy of American parents, he was home schooled by his parents before entering The Ecole des Beaux-Arts at the age of 18.

Gustav Klimt 1862 (Austria)-1918
Founder of the Vienna Sezession School (Art Nouveau).

Maurice Utrillo 1883 (France)-1955
Born in Montmarte, Paris. He took the name Utrillo, having been encouraged to do so by an art critic of that name.

Q: In what year did Richard Nixon resign?

Famous **Authors**
and their Books

Emily Bronte	Wuthering Heights
Truman Capote	In Cold Blood
Rachel Carlson	Silent Spring
Willa Cather	My Antonia
James Fenimore Cooper	The Last of The Mohicans The Deerslayer The Prairie The Pioneers (Leatherstocking Tales)
Stephen Crane	The Red Badge of Courage

Charles Dickens	A Tale of Two Cities (French Revolution) Martin Chuzzlewit The Pickwick Papers Nicholas Nickelby Great Expectations David Copperfield A Christmas Carol
Fyodor Dostoyevsky	Crime and Punishment
Sir Arthur Conan Doyle	Sherlock Holmes Series
Theodore Dreiser	An American Tragedy Sister Cary The Titan The Financier
Edna Ferber	Giant (A book about Texas)
F. Scott Fitzgerald	The Great Gatsby Tender Is The Night This Side of Paradise The Beautiful and The Damned
John Galsworthy	The Forsythe Saga The Island Pharisees The Man of Property
Nathaniel Hawthorne	The Scarlet Letter The House of Seven Gables
Ernest Hemingway	For Whom The Bells Tolls (WWI) The Sun Also Rises The Old Man and The Sea A Farewell To Arms
Victor Hugo	Les Miserables
James Joyce	Ulysses
Franz Kafka	Meditation The Judgment The Metamorphosis

Q: Which two Vice Presidents resigned?

David Kahn	The Code-Breakers
	Hitler's Spies
David McCullough	Truman
	John Adams
Herman Melville	Moby Dick
	Typee
	Omoo
	Billy Budd
Margaret Mitchell	Gone With The Wind (Civil War)
Eugene O'Neill	The Iceman Cometh (a play)
Erich Maria Remarque	All Quiet on The Western Front (WW I)
John Steinbeck	The Grapes of Wrath
	Travels with Charlie
	Cannery Row
	Of Mice and Men
Irwin Shaw	Winds of War (WW II)
	Young Lions (WW II)
William Thackerey	Vanity Fair
Leo Tolstoy	War and Peace
	Anna Karenina
	Death of Ivan Ilyich
Anthony Trollope	The Prime Minister
	The Eustace Diamonds
	The Warden
	Phinneas Finn
	(many others)
Kurt Vonnegut	Slaughterhouse-Five
	Cat's Cradle
Franz Werfel	The Forty Days of Musa Dagh

Edith Wharton	Ethan Frome The House of Mirth The Age of Innocence
Theodore H. White	The Making of The President In Search of History
Oscar Wilde	The Picture of Dorian Grey The Importance of Being Ernest (a play)
Thorton Wilder	The Bridge of San Luis Rey Our Town (a play)
Herman Wouk	Majorie Morningstar The Caine Mutiny

Q: Name the French King who was guillotined in 1793.

Musical Instruments
By Type

Woodwinds

Bassoon

Clarinet

Flute

Oboe

Piccolo

Saxophone

Although made of brass, it is considered a woodwind. The mouthpiece is similar to that of the Clarinet

Brass

Baritone Horn

Bugle

Cornet

Euphonium

Flugelhorn

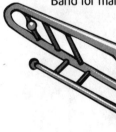

A big Bugle with valves. More mellow.

French Horn

Sousaphone

A big brass bass with the horn upright. Named after its developer, John Philip Sousa, a noted composer of band music. Sousa was the band leader of the Marine Corps Band for many years.

Tenor Horn

Trumpet

Trombone

Tuba

String

Violin

The most famous Violin is the Stradivarius, made by Antonio Stradivari. Worth well over $1 million. Stradivari died in Cremora, Italy in 1737.

Viola

Cello   (Violincello)

Bass   (Bass violin)

Harp

Percussion

Vibraphone   Similar to a Xylophone

Kettle Drum

Snare Drum

Triangle

Cymbal

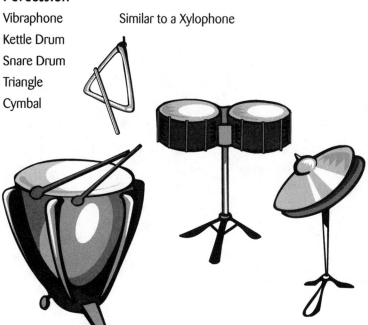

Q: Which planet is the smallest in diameter?

Roman Numerals

Developed and used in ancient Rome to indicate a numeric value. There are occasional questions in trivia games regarding Roman numerals. Easy to learn and remember!

A letter stood for a value as follows:

I = 1
V = 5
X = 10
L = 50
C = 100
D = 500
M = 1000

I = 1	VI = 6	XI = 11
II = 2	VII = 7	XII = 12
III = 3	VIII = 8	XIII = 13
IV = 4	IX = 9	XIV = 14
V = 5	X = 10	XV = 15

Put them together like this:

VI = 6   which is 5 (V) + 1 (I) = 6
IV = 4   which is 5 (V) - 1 (I) = 4

(1 subtracted from 5. Subtract if a letter representing smaller number precedes a letter representing a larger one)

More examples

XXIV = 24   Addition and Subtraction! 20 + 4, where IV = 4

ML = 1050

MDL = 1550

CM = 900   Remember Subtraction: 1000 − 100 = 900

The price, in cents, of a bottle of MillerLite® at various places:

Starland	(Washington, DC)	CD	400 cents
Fast Eddies	(Washington, DC)	CCL	250 cents
North Star	(Allegany County, NY)	CCXXV	225 cents
Hog Heaven	(Islamorada Key, FL)	CCL	250 cents
Rafter's	(Amherst, MA)	CCLXXV	275 cents

Note that these are all happy hour prices!

'MillerLite" is a trademark of the Miller Brewing company, Milwaukee, WI.

Q: Name the world's largest city.

Wine

This page is not for wine drinking BAR GAME players who are familiar with the subject. The information contained here is for BAR GAME players who want to be better informed about wine in order to have a chance at a correct answer on a question about wine.

Wines are generally named after either the grape from which the wine is made, or from the region in which the wine comes from.

Champagne, from the Pinot Noir grape, is named after a region of France in which it is made.

In France, the wine must be 100% from the grape after which it is named. In California, only 75% of the named grape is required.

Here is a list of well known grapes from which wine is made and some brief comments about them.

White Wines named after the grape used to make them

Reisling	Wines from the Rhine and Moselle valleys use this wine
Chardonnay	Grown world wide
Gewurztraminer	A spicy wine grown in the cooler regions of France, Germany and the USA
Savignon Blanc	Grown widely in New Zealand
Chenin Blanc	Grown in California and the Loire Valley in France
Verdicchio	Grown exclusively in Italy – very delicate
Sylvaner	From the cooler part of Germany – low in acidity

Red Wines named for the grape used to create them

Merlot	Grown in California, France and USA

St. Francis Reserve is considered my many connoisseurs to be the finest of the many excellent California Merlots.

Cabernet Savignon	Frequently blended with Merlot
Gagnolino	Another wine from the Piedmont
Doletto	From the Italian Piedmont – consumed fresh without ageing
Pinotage	Grows in South Africa – a cross between Pinot Noir and Cinsault

Wines named after the region of origin

Bordeaux	Bordeaux region of France
Chianti	Chianti region of Italy
Beaujolais	
Chablis	
Burgundy	

Q: Which state was the first to let women vote?

Some wines just have names

Liebfraumilch	Milk from the Virgin
Chateau Neuf de Pape	Chateau of The New Pope
Blue Nun	
Chateau-Lafite Rothschild	Chateau-Lafite owned by Rothschild family

One of the most well known wines in the world is Chateau Lafite-Rothschild, a Bordeau. The vineyards at Chateau Lafite in the Bordeau region of France have been owned by The Rothschild family about 200 years. A very fine wine.

There is also a Mouton Rothschild, considered by many to be the equal of Lafite. The grapes for this wine are grown on the French estate of the English branch of the Rothschild family, distant relatives of the French family.

Wine Bottle Size

A Standard Bottle contains   750 milliliters

Half bottle   375 milliliters

Split   ¼ bottle

Bigger Bottles

Name	size in bottles	Named for
Magnum	2	Means 'Big'
Jeroboam	4	A contemporary of King Solomon 1000 BC
Methuselah	8	Biblical figure from Genesis. He lived 1000 years. I hope he used Botox!
Salmanazar	12	An Assyrian King circa 500 BC
Balthazar	16	Balthazar, Melchior, and Jaspar were the 3 Kings to visit Bethlehem
Nebuchadnezzar	20	King of Babylon 600 BC

Nebuchadnezzars of Champagne are for real party people!

Split   Half   Standard Bottle   Magnum   Jeroboam   Methusalem   Salmanazar   Balthazar   Nebuchadnezzar

Q: Which planet is nearest the sun?

Mushrooms

Mushrooms are fungi, not plants. There are over 2000 varieties. Many are poisonous but mycologists love them all!

The most prominent edible mushrooms are:

Name	Description
Button	Also known as the White Button. In all grocery stores
Beech	Small, light brown in color - sweet
Black Trumpet	Lily Shaped
Chantorelle	Elegant looking. Shaped like a vase
Cremini	A small mushroom with a brown cap
Enoki	Dainty with an elongated 'O" shape
Hedgehog	Orange-yellow color
Maitake	Brown color
Matsutake	Pine mushroom
Morel	Spongy and hallow dark brown in color
Oyster	Fan shaped
Porcini	Bulbous stem - called a "Polish mushroom"
Portabella	A mature cremini
Shiitake	Brown in color, called an "Oak Mushroom"
Truffle	The most expensive. Found in France. $900 per pound
Woodear	A mushroom found in China
Yellow Foot	Brown in color

Residences
Of Note

Residence	Location	Home Of
Blenheim	UK	Winston Churchill
Biltmore	Asheville, SC	George Vanderbilt
Breakers	Newport, RI	Cornelius Vanderbilt
Buckingham Palace	London, UK	Queen of England
Crawford Ranch	TX	George W. Bush
10 Downing Street	London	UK Prime Minister's House
Falling Water House	PA	Designed by Frank Lloyd Wright
Hermitage	TN	Andrew Jackson
Hyde Park	NY	Franklin D. Roosevelt
Gettysburg Farm	PA	Dwight D. Eisenhower
Kinderhook	NY	Martin Van Buren
Olana	NY	Frederick Church (artist)

Q: Who wrote "The Great Gatsby"?

Monticello	VA	Thomas Jefferson
Montpelier	VA	James Madison
Mount Vernon	VA	George Washington
1600 Pennsylvania Avenue	Washington, DC	The White House
Perdernales Ranch	TX	Lyndon B. Johnson
Pocantico Hills	NY	John D. Rockefeller & heirs
Sagamore Hill	Oyster Bay, NY	Theodore Roosevelt
San Simeon	CA	William Randolph Hearst
Tsarskyo Selo	St. Petersburg	Tsar's Village
Topkapi	Istanbul	Ottoman Sultan's Palace
Valkill	Hyde Park, NY	Eleanor Roosevelt
Versailles	France	Louis XIV's Palace
Winter Palace	St. Petersburg	Tsar's Palace

Fictional Residences

Scarlet Ohara - Gone With The Wind	Tara Plantation Atlanta, GA
Batman (Bruce Wayne)	'Stately' Wayne Manor
Sherlock Holmes	221-B Baker Street (London)
The Munsters - TV 1970's	1313 Mockingbird Lane
The Simpson's - TV	742 Evergreeen Terrace
Archie Bunker - TV	704 Hauser Street, Queens, NY
Seinfeld - TV	129 West 81st Street, NYC
Everyone Loves Raymond	320 Fowler, Lynbrook, NY (Long Island)
Cheers	112½ Beacon Street, Boston Modeled after a real bar, Bull and Finch Pub 84 Beacon Street, Boston

Mork & Mindy	1619 Pine Street, Boulder, CO
The Huxtable's (The Bill Cosby Show)	10 Stigwood Avenue, Brooklyn, NY
Richie Cunningham (Fonzie's friend)	179 Ridge Street, Milwaukee, WI
The Brady Bunch	4222 Clinton Way, Westdale, CA
The Odd Couple	1049 Park Avenue, New York City
The Honeymooners (Jackie Gleason starred as Ralph Kramden)	328 Chauncey Street, Brooklyn, NY
Leave It To Beaver (Ward and June Cleaver - sons Wally and 'Beaver', Theodore)	211 Pine Street – first two seasons 485 Maple Street, Mayfield, USA
Dallas	Southfork RanchTexas
Dynasty (The Carrington's)	173 Essex Drive, Denver, CO

Q: In what year was Julius Caesar assassinated?

MEGATOUCH

Megatouch—Introduction

The MEGATOUCH game, manufactured by Merit Industries in Reading, Pennsylvania is a common sight on the bar in thousands of pubs across America.

The game is undergoing continual improvement and change with new games being added on a regular basis. It is a real test of a players eye-hand coordination and intelligence.

It is a great social experience, playing against another person or playing with a partner against the machine.

Some of the games require previous knowledge of the game that MEGATOUCH simulates. Hearts, a very popular card game, is difficult for a person to play if he has not actually played the game with real playing cards. Same with Backgammon and Chess.

Most of the games are easy to learn and the player can be an expert after a few games. BOXXI, a game where the player removes boxes by touching the screen, can be learned almost instantly.

ELEVEN-UP is also very easy to learn. In this game, cards are removed from the screen by touching cards whose value totals eleven.

All require fairly quick reaction, and some are genuinely habit forming.

Sit down it front of the MEGATOUCH, put in a dollar or two, and test your skills against the machine, or against other players.

Zip 21 and Black Jack

ZIP 21 is a variation of Black Jack, the gambling game played at all casinos. The object of ZIP 21 is to add cards to a hand so that the sum of the values equals 21.

Zip 21 Game Description

A 52 card deck appears on the top left of the screen with the first card visible. Four hands are displayed in the center of the screen where the player will place a card, by touching the card and the hand that he wishes to put it in.

On the top of each hand in the center of the screen is a box where the sum of the value of the cards in that hand are displayed.

If the first card on the deck is a '10', it would be placed in the first hand. If the next card displayed is an 'A', the player would put it in the same hand as the '10'. This adds up to 21, and the hand is cleared and points are awarded to the player for this win.

If the first card is an 'A' and the subsequent card is not a 10, the player should put the subsequent card in another hand and await a 10 to appear to play in the ace. This strategy is advisable because in a deck of 52 cards, 16 cards carry the value 10. (4 Kings, 4 Queens, 4 Jacks, and 4 10s.)

No card can be put in a hand if the sum of the cards in the hand total over 21. Four cards can be skipped in the course of the play. The game ends when all hands cannot be added to because the sum would exceed 21, or, the 52 card deck is finished. If the deck is finished, a bonus is awarded. A hand that contains 5 cards below 21 is also a winner.

Strategy
A standard 52 card deck is used in this game. So, if you have a super memory you will remember what cards are left in the deck. Very difficult.

An attempt should be made to have all hands being played having a different sum so that there will be a greater opportunity to get a card that will result in a 21 for one of the hands.

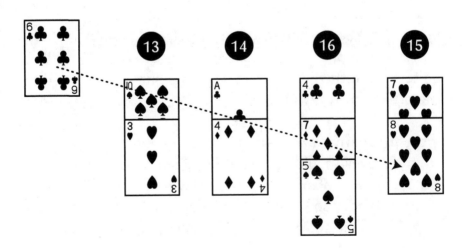

For example, if four hands are 13, 14, 15, and 16, if the next card is an 8, 7, 6, or 5, a win will result as one of the hands can be made a 21. Therefore, a new card should not be added to one of the hands if the resultant sum is equal to the value of one of the existing hands.

A card should not be added to a hand if another card of the same value will be needed to get a 21 for that hand. For example, if a hand has a total of 13, never add a 4 to it because another 4 would be needed to get to 21.

Black Jack

Playing against a dealer, the object of Black Jack is to have the sum of the cards dealt to you be under or equal but not over 21. If the cards dealt to you total over 21, the hand is a 'bust' and you automatically lose even if the dealer subsequently 'busts' as well.

Two cards are dealt to you initially and additional cards are requested from the dealer. When you are satisfied with your hand, the dealer will then play his hand. When your first two cards are an Ace and a face card or a ten, you have a black jack and you win without the dealer playing his hand. Face cards are worth 10, an ace is worth one or eleven, other cards carry their numeric value.

Eleven Up

Twenty two cards are displayed in a double pyramid pattern on the screen. One card is displayed at the bottom of the pyramid.

Object
The object of this game is to remove cards from the screen by touching a group of cards in the two pyramids that add up to eleven. Any card that is not covered by another card can be used in addition to the card at the bottom.

If a group whose sum is 11 is not on the screen, the bottom card is touched, it is moved to the screen and another card from the 'deck' replaces it.

A group, whose value adds to eleven, can consist of two or more cards. To play this game and get a high score, it is best to know the combinations that add up to 11 and move quickly to touch them as time is relevant in this game.

Combinations adding to eleven are as follows:

Ace + 10	Ace + 2 + 8
2 + 9	Ace + 3 + 7
3 + 8	Ace + 3 + 5 + 2
4 + 7	Ace + 4 + 5 + Ace
5 + 6	etc

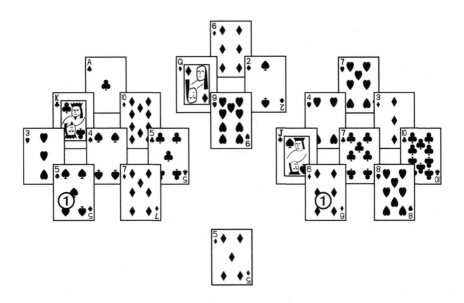

Speed is important. The game is terminated even if you are not finished after an allotted period of time.

Strategy

Always play cards on the pyramid in preference to playing the card at the bottom. If a 5 and 6 is playable on the pyramid and a 5 is at the bottom of the screen, play the 5 on the pyramid rather than the 5 on the bottom. This will maximize your score.

Wild Eights

(A variation of the child's card game, Crazy Eights)

The game is played with a full deck of 52 cards with the 'eights' being wild. Wild means that they may be used as a card of any value or suit. Five cards are displayed at the bottom of the screen. Each card that is displayed is to be removed to one of three stacks in the middle of the screen. To place a card on one of the stacks, it must match in suit or value of the card that is on the top of that stack.

Each stack awards a different value when a card is placed there. If a card the matches the value of the card on the top of that stack, the score value is increased as follows:

The left most stack starts at 500 and increases by 500 each time a card match occurs. The stacks in the middle and to the right start at 200 and 100 respectively and increase in amounts of 200 and 100 if a value of card match occurs.

Strategy
The critical part of this game is to maximize the number of value matches to increase the score awarded.

To maximize the score, concentrate on the left most stack as it awards the highest number of points. All matching cards should be played there, if possible.

Example:

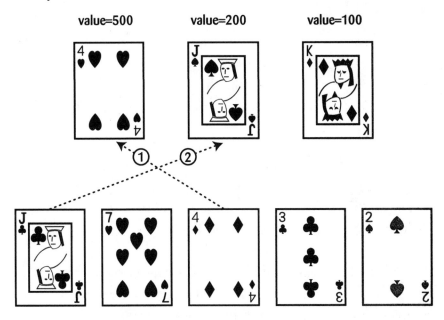

value=500   value=200   value=100

Play the table 4 on the stack 4. The Jack on the second stack increases the value of additional cards on that stack by 200 while the addition of the 4 on the first stack increases the score value of that stack by 500. Wait for the new card to replace the 4 before playing again.

A **Wild Eight** left on the deck part awards a bonus of 10,000, 20,000 and 40,000 if left there at the end of the hand.

Time is of the essence in this game. Best to act on instinct. If you think too much, the **times up** flag will come on.

Quintzee

Quintzee is a game very similar to the board game, Yahtzee. Ergo, Yahtzee lovers, go down to the local pub to enjoy a bottle of MillerLite® and to be challenged by Quintzee.

For those readers who are not familiar with Yahtzee, learn it from a friend and then play Quintzee on the Maxx machine. It is easy to learn but a description of the game is long winded and is not included here.

There are a few minor differences in the two games. Quintzee does not offer a small straight (four numbers in a row on the five dice) and does give a bonus if all of the combinations (three, four, five of a kind, any, full house, and straight) are attained.

Strategy
The bonus that is rewarded is the most important aspect of this game. Namely, over 63 in the 1 to 6 boxes and fill in all the score boxes in 7 thru 12.

Best to try for the most difficult combinations first, the five of a kind, the straight, and the full house. The number of 1's and 2's should not be filled in until the end of the game when they can be used as a 'throw away' for an attempt to make a straight, etc that failed. Any is also used as a last resort item.

Nancy Travern, Proprietor of Nancy's North Star, one of the finest pubs in Allegany County, NY, is a 'World Class' Quintzee player. Her skills have been honed by playing many games during the slow period between lunch and the cocktail hour.

When the night bartender comes in at 8pm, Nancy frequently stays at work to enjoy a few games of Quintzee. Now off duty, she can enjoy a bottle or two of her favorite beer while playing. (Or maybe a martini)

   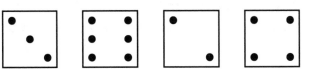

Tritop

Tritop is a fast moving game, simple to play. A real test for quick reflexes. A 'three top pyramid' of 28 cards is displayed with only the bottom row of 10 cards facing up. Above that are three more rows of face down cards containing, from bottom up, 9 cards, 6 cards, and 3 cards.

Twenty three cards are stacked at the bottom with the first card showing. This is the called the 'card stack'.

The object of the game is to remove all the cards from the pyramid, by touching those that are, in value, one above or one below the card showing at the top of the 'stack' on the bottom.

When the 'stack card' does not match (one higher or one lower) a face up card on the pyramid, another stack card is turned over by touching it. The round is completed when all twenty three stack cards are played. The first pyramid cleared scores 5,000, the second 10,000 and the third 15,000.

Speed is essential as 80 seconds are allowed to complete a round.

When a card is matched, and removed from the pyramid, it is placed, face up, On the top of the stack at the bottom.

It then becomes the card to be used for matching and removal of additional cards on the pyramid.

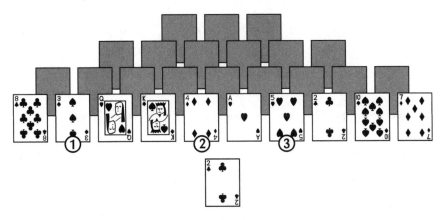

Therefore, if a 2 is face up on the bottom and a 3, 4, and 5 are face up on the pyramid, all three can be removed by touching the 3 first. This becomes the key card at the bottom. Touching the 4 will remove the 4 and place that below. Then the 5 is touched and removed and the 5 is placed below as the case card. If there is no 4 or 6 on the pyramid now, the 5 at the bottom is touched and another card from the twenty three card stack is shown. If this card cannot be matched, it is to be touched and another card revealed. The game is over when all 23 cards on the stack are played.

Strategy
The basic strategy in this game is to look for a series of cards to remove from the pyramid. For example, if the stack card is a 5, look for a 5, 6, 7 to remove or a 4, 3, 2 to remove. Scan all pyramids looking for these series.

Crazy **Hearts**

Hearts is a card game familiar to many. Played with a 52 card deck, 13 are dealt to each player. Each player passes three cards to another player before the play begins.

This game on NTN is exactly the same as the card game, brilliantly designed with excellent visuals. It is very easy to play.

The hand that holds the deuce of clubs initiates the play by leading that card. Each player plays a card from the same suit that was led. If a player cannot follow suit, he may play any card in his hand. Hearts cannot be led until a heart has been played.

Each heart won in a trick counts one against you and the Queen of Spades counts thirteen against you, **except** if you take all the hearts and the Queen of Clubs in which case you are awarded minus 26 points. This coup of taking all the hearts and the queen of Spades is called 'shooting the moon'.

Strategy
Always try to **shoot the moon** which is taking all the hearts and the Queen of Spades. It is easy to do as the computer program that you are playing against does not sense the 'Moon Shot' taking place in many cases.

This is a fast paced game. Doubly enjoyed when your other hand is holding a bottle of cold brew.

Checkerz

This is the same game as Checkers, called Draughts in England.

My grandmother taught me to play checkers when I was about five years old. She usually let me win so I would maintain an interest.

Not so with the computer program on the Megatouch Checkerz game. I have rarely seen the computer lose. It is almost undefeated.

The best way to play is to allow the computer to jump you in a way that allows you to jump right back. Trade checkers in order to simplify the game somewhat. Do not move the back row until you are forced to. If you fail to jump the opponent when the opportunity presents itself, you lose the piece. Ergo, be careful.

Contact our publisher, New Chapter Press, if you know of a Checkers expert who can regularly beat this game. We will include his methodology in the next edition.

An easy way to win a drink or two at your favorite pub. Bet someone that the computer can beat them playing Checkers. You will rarely lose.

Boxxi

Object
Object of the game is to remove, by touching, adjacent boxes of the same color from the screen.

How To Play
A very simple game, requiring little concentration. So relax and order MillerLite® to enjoy while playing. One hand on the bottle of a cold draft, the other playing the game.

No one seems comfortable playing Megatouch with two hands. Why?

Green, blue, red, tan boxes are displayed on the screen. Touch two or more adjacent boxes of the same color, therefore removing them from the screen. The game ends when all boxes are removed or when there are no more boxes of the same color that are adjacent.

Scoring
Higher scores result when a touch removes a high number of boxes at the same time. For example, removing two boxes will give a score less than removing ten boxes with one touch. A bonus is awarded depending on the

percentage of boxes removed, with all removed being the largest bonus given.

Strategy

Look at the screen and determine which color is the least prevalent. Start with that color. Remove boxes as many boxes of that color as possible. However, be careful that a removal does not disturb a adjacent group above the one that you are removing. Remove the one of the top first.

When all of the first color are removed, then start with the least prevalent of the remaining colors.

When that color's removal has been completed, look for any remaining first color boxes that may have been joined. Remove them. Continue the removal, removing the colors that are least prevalent first. **A high score will result.**

Pixie Lynn, a waitress at Fast Eddie's on K Street in Washington, is the best player the author has seen. It is rumored that George Bush's daughters have seen her play there when they visited The White House, which is two blocks from Fast Eddies.

The game is similar to the game "Collapse", available on Yahoo and on CD's for your PC. But play this game at your favorite pub while enjoying a cold draft. Playing on your PC at home is for weenies!

Photo Hunt

Photo Hunt is a really fun game for one, two or a group of players.

Two photos of the same scene are displayed. There are almost imperceptible differences in the two pictures. The object of the game is to identify the differences in the two pictures and touch that spot on one of the pictures that is different. These differences are to be identified by touching the screen at that spot of the discrepancy. Each picture has five differences. The number of points obtained is based on the number found.

For example, a table might be part of the scene. One might have one leg missing. A window pane might have part of the frame missing or slightly different. A landscape scene might have one shrub missing in one of the pictures. If a house is pictured with two chimneys, the other picture might have only one chimney.

It is best to have at least one male and one female player when playing this game. The female brain and the male brain react differently to these puzzles. Women and men always find different discrepancies. It seems that this game is played better by female players! Perhaps they have a better attention to detail. Challenge the men, ladies. Show them your superiority!

Pub Quiz

Pub Quiz - A Great Game

The PUB QUIZ is a new game that is appearing in upscale pubs and private clubs throughout the USA.

It is played the old fashioned way with questions asked by a Master of Ceremonies. Answers are written on paper score sheets.

The questions, score sheets, and answers are provided by subscription from Brainstormers, based in San Francisco. Their web site, www.brainstormers.com, provides the details.

The players at the pub pair up as teams and confer before writing the answer on the score sheet. Usually four people comprise a team.

It is a great social scene which attracts a young crowd of well educated people, many with high IQ's and are proud of it.

The competition is usually quite intense and all team conferences are conducted in great secrecy by whispering to prevent the team sitting at the next table from over hearing their discussion.

Venues where the game is played are available on the web site.

History of the Pub Quiz

Cultural anthropologists are still debating the precise origins of today's hugely popular Pub Quiz, a 'live' trivia quiz show administered by a 'Quizmaster' to teams of bar goers everywhere. Traditionally scheduled for an 'off' night (usually Sunday – Thursday), the Pub Quiz is a revenue boon for bar and clubs. It provides lively entertainment in a friendly, social atmosphere for anyone old enough to go to a bar.

Though the truth is still shrouded in a barroom haze, most likely the Pub Quiz evolved in Britain and Ireland in the early days of television. Pubs, of course, have always been places to drink, socialize and relax. But in the 1950s, many pubs had another draw: unlike most homes, the pubs had television. Televised game shows in particular drew great attention of the imbibers. Pub regulars often called out answers to game show questions before the studio contestants did, prompting fellow pub goers to shout, 'Why don't you go on that show?' to the most knowledgeable bar 'contestants.'

The friendly rivalry, lighthearted banter and increased bar business attributable to the television quiz shows inspired pub owners to offer 'live' quiz shows as a regular feature on their pub entertainment calendars. At one point, as many as 500 teams competed in weekly inter-pub matches in Lancashire County, England. To this day 'live' quiz shows enjoy immense popularity throughout Britain and Ireland.

In the United States, Pub Quiz Shows thrive in San Francisco, Boston, Chicago and other cities. Venues host weekly Pub Trivia Quiz Shows, packing the house with trivia fans eager to show their prowess. Teams formed of friends, co-workers, family (and even the occasional single person at the bar) battle each other over rounds of questions fired at them by the host or pub 'Quizmaster'.

Brainstormer Pub Quiz® Today

Brainstormer Pub Quiz® was founded in San Francisco in 1996 by Liam McAtasney, a native of County Armagh, N. Ireland. Brainstormer supplies total trivia Quiz Packs to bars, private clubs, corporate clients and businesses across the United States. These Quiz Packs enable the venues to host their own fun, 'LIVE' trivia events.

Besides offering a great way to meet new people (including members of the opposite sex!), the Brainstormer Pub Quiz® invites participants to flex their trivia muscles and perhaps even win a prize or two. You can find a venue near you by logging onto http://www.brainstormer.com/location.asp, which has a list of venues in the United States as well as information on hosting your own event down at your local!

Trivia Review

Name the two Vice Presidents who resigned.

SPIRO AGNEW

JOHN C. CALHOUN

Who was the King of Babylon in 600 BC for whom a wine bottle is named?

NEBUCHADNEZAR

Who was the only bachelor President?

JAMES BUCHANAN

Who painted the Sistine Chapel in Rome?

MICHELANGELO

Name a book by Ernest Hemingway.

A FAREWELL TO ARMS

THE SUN ALSO RISES

THE OLD MAN AND THE SEA

FOR WHOM THE BELL TOLLS

Who was the youngest American Vice President?

JOHN BRECKINRIDGE (VP FOR BUCHANAN)

Which is the largest planet?

JUPITER

Which California Merlot is considered to be the finest by many connoisseurs?

ST. FRANCIS RESERVE

Who was assassinated in 44 BC?

JULIUS CAESAR (BY BRUTUS)

Who wrote the play "Our Town"?

THORTON WILDER

Who was defeated at Waterloo in 1814 by Wellington?

NAPOLEON

Who was the first President born in the USA.

MARTIN VAN BUREN

Who was the first President to die in Office?

WILLIAM HENRY HARRISON

Who gave the "I Have A Dream" speech in Washington DC in 1963?

MARTIN LUTHER KING

How many times was English King, Henry VIII, married?

SIX

Name the Capital and Nickname of New York State?

ALBANY & THE EMPIRE STATE

Jackson Pollock was a member of what school of artists?

THE ABSTRACT IMPRESSIONISTS (NEW YORK SCHOOL)

Who wrote the book, "The Scarlet Letter"?

NATHANIEL HAWTHORNE

Name a book by John Steinbeck.

TRAVELS WITH CHARLIE

THE GRAPES OF WRATH

CANNERY ROW

OF MICE AND MEN

Who painted "Mona Lisa", now on display in The Louvre.

LEONARDO DA VINCI

Which state was the first to allow women to vote?

WYOMING

What is the home address of the following:

British Prime Minister?

10 DOWNING STREET, LONDON

Seinfeld?

129 WEST 81ST STREET , NYC

Sherlock Holmes?

221-B BAKER STREET , LONDON

When was the first moon landing?

JULY, 1969

Index